MY Travel Journal

_____'s Travel Journal

I AM GOING TO _____

I AM TRAVELING WITH _____

_____

I WILL BE AWAY FOR _____

_____

TRAVEL TIMELINE

Write Where you went and What you did in each block below.

DAY 1

DAY 2

DAY 3

DAY 4

DAY 5

DAY 6

DAY 7

MY PACKING LIST

WHAT I MUST TAKE...

○ _____

○ _____

○ _____

○ _____

○ _____

○ _____

○ _____

○ _____

○ _____

○ _____

○ _____

○ _____

○ _____

○ _____

○ _____

○ _____

○ _____

○ _____

MY PACKING LIST

WHAT I WOULD LIKE TO TAKE...

MY FRIENDS

Name _____
Address _____
_____
Phone _____
Email _____

Name _____
Address _____
_____
Phone _____
Email _____

Name _____
Address _____
_____
Phone _____
Email _____

Name _____
Address _____
_____
Phone _____
Email _____

Name _____
Address _____
_____
Phone _____
Email _____

Name _____
Address _____
_____
Phone _____
Email _____

Name _____
Address _____
_____
Phone _____
Email _____

Name _____
Address _____
_____
Phone _____
Email _____

MY FRIENDS

Name_____

Address_____

_____

Phone_____

Email_____

Name_____

Address_____

_____

Phone_____

Email_____

Name_____

Address_____

_____

Phone_____

Email_____

Name_____

Address_____

_____

Phone_____

Email_____

Name_____

Address_____

_____

Phone_____

Email_____

Name_____

Address_____

_____

Phone_____

Email_____

Name_____

Address_____

_____

Phone_____

Email_____

Name_____

Address_____

_____

Phone_____

Email_____

TRIP DAY 1

Weather:

☐ ☀ ☐ ⛅ ☐ ☁ ☐ 🌧 ☐ 🌨

Today I Feel

😊 😐 ☹

DRAW SOMETHING FROM THE DAY!

WHAT DID I DO TODAY

_____
_____
_____
_____
_____
_____
_____
_____
_____

BEST PART

_____
_____
_____
_____
_____
_____
_____
_____
_____

Date .... LOCATION ....

I stayed at ....

I traveled by ....

FIRST TIME EVER

_____
_____
_____
_____
_____
_____
_____
_____
_____
_____

WHAT I SAW

_____
_____
_____
_____
_____
_____
_____
_____
_____
_____

BEST FOOD I ATE TODAY

_____
_____
_____
_____
_____
_____
_____
_____
_____

TODAY BEST MOMENT

_____
_____
_____
_____
_____
_____
_____
_____
_____

TODAY'S FAVORITE MEMORY

A COOL THING ABOUT TODAY

TRIP DAY 2

Weather:

☐ ☐ ☐ ☐ ☐

Today I Feel

🙂 😐 ☹️

DRAW SOMETHING FORM THE DAY!

WHAT DID I DO TODAY

_____
_____
_____
_____
_____
_____
_____
_____
_____

BEST PART

_____
_____
_____
_____
_____
_____
_____
_____
_____

Date .... LOCATION ....

I stayed at ....

I traveled by ....

FIRST TIME EVER

_____
_____
_____
_____
_____
_____
_____
_____
_____

WHAT I SAW

_____
_____
_____
_____
_____
_____
_____
_____
_____

BEST FOOD I ATE TODAY

_____
_____
_____
_____
_____
_____
_____
_____
_____

TODAY BEST MOMENT

_____
_____
_____
_____
_____
_____
_____
_____
_____

TODAY'S FAVORITE MEMORY

A COOL THING ABOUT TODAY

TRIP DAY 3

Weather:

☐ ☐ ☐ ☐ ☐

Today I Feel

DRAW SOMETHING FROM THE DAY!

WHAT DID I DO TODAY

_____
_____
_____
_____
_____
_____
_____
_____
_____

BEST PART

_____
_____
_____
_____
_____
_____
_____
_____
_____

Date .... LOCATION ....

I stayed at ....
I traveled by ....

FIRST TIME EVER

_____
_____
_____
_____
_____
_____
_____
_____
_____

WHAT I SAW

_____
_____
_____
_____
_____
_____
_____
_____
_____

BEST FOOD I ATE TODAY

_____
_____
_____
_____
_____
_____
_____
_____
_____
_____

TODAY BEST MOMENT

_____
_____
_____
_____
_____
_____
_____
_____
_____
_____

TODAY'S FAVORITE MEMORY

A COOL THING ABOUT TODAY

TRIP DAY 4

Weather:

☐ ☀ ☐ ⛅ ☐ ☁ ☐ ⛈ ☐ 🌨

Today I Feel

😊 😐 ☹

DRAW SOMETHING FROM THE DAY!

WHAT DID I DO TODAY

BEST PART

Date .... LOCATION ....

I stayed at ....

I traveled by ....

FIRST TIME EVER

_____
_____
_____
_____
_____
_____
_____
_____
_____

WHAT I SAW

_____
_____
_____
_____
_____
_____
_____
_____
_____

BEST FOOD I ATE TODAY

_____
_____
_____
_____
_____
_____
_____
_____
_____

TODAY BEST MOMENT

_____
_____
_____
_____
_____
_____
_____
_____
_____

TODAY'S FAVORITE MEMORY

A COOL THING ABOUT TODAY

TRIP DAY 5

Weather:

☐ ☐ ☐ ☐ ☐

DRAW SOMETHING FROM THE DAY!

WHAT DID I DO TODAY

_____
_____
_____
_____
_____
_____
_____
_____
_____

BEST PART

_____
_____
_____
_____
_____
_____
_____
_____
_____
_____

Date _____ LOCATION _____

I stayed at _____

I traveled by _____

FIRST TIME EVER

_____
_____
_____
_____
_____
_____
_____
_____
_____

WHAT I SAW

_____
_____
_____
_____
_____
_____
_____
_____
_____
_____
_____

BEST FOOD I ATE TODAY

_____
_____
_____
_____
_____
_____
_____
_____
_____

TODAY BEST MOMENT

_____
_____
_____
_____
_____
_____
_____
_____
_____

TODAY'S FAVORITE MEMORY

A COOL THING ABOUT TODAY

TRIP DAY 6

Weather:

☐ ☀ ☐ ⛅ ☐ ☁ ☐ 🌧 ☐ 🌨

🙂 😐 ☹

DRAW SOMETHING FROM THE DAY!

WHAT DID I DO TODAY

_____
_____
_____
_____
_____
_____
_____
_____
_____

BEST PART

_____
_____
_____
_____
_____
_____
_____
_____

Date .... LOCATION ....

I stayed at ....
I traveled by ....

FIRST TIME EVER

_____
_____
_____
_____
_____
_____
_____
_____
_____

WHAT I SAW

_____
_____
_____
_____
_____
_____
_____
_____
_____

BEST FOOD I ATE TODAY

_____
_____
_____
_____
_____
_____
_____
_____

TODAY BEST MOMENT

_____
_____
_____
_____
_____
_____
_____
_____

TODAY'S FAVORITE MEMORY

A COOL THING ABOUT TODAY

TRIP DAY 7

Weather:

☐ ☐ ☐ ☐ ☐

😊 😐 ☹️

DRAW SOMETHING FROM THE DAY!

WHAT DID I DO TODAY

_____
_____
_____
_____
_____
_____
_____
_____
_____

BEST PART

_____
_____
_____
_____
_____
_____
_____
_____

Date .... LOCATION ....

I stayed at ....
I traveled by ....

FIRST TIME EVER

_____
_____
_____
_____
_____
_____
_____
_____
_____

WHAT I SAW

_____
_____
_____
_____
_____
_____
_____
_____
_____

BEST FOOD I ATE TODAY

_____
_____
_____
_____
_____
_____
_____
_____

TODAY BEST MOMENT

_____
_____
_____
_____
_____
_____
_____
_____

TODAY'S FAVORITE MEMORY

A COOL THING ABOUT TODAY

SOME OTHER MEMORIES OF MY TRIP

PHOTO / STICKER

PHOTO / STICKER

PHOTO / STICKER

PHOTO / STICKER

PHOTO / STICKER

PHOTO / STICKER

PHOTO / STICKER

PHOTO / STICKER

PHOTO / STICKER

PHOTO / STICKER

PHOTO / STICKER

PHOTO / STICKER

PHOTO / STICKER

PHOTO / STICKER

PHOTO / STICKER

PHOTO / STICKER

PHOTO / STICKER

PHOTO / STICKER

CPSIA information can be obtained
at www.ICGtesting.com
Printed in the USA
LVOW09s0509141217
559613LV00017BA/233/P

9 781979 644341